There are hundreds
and hundreds of reasons
why this book had to
be written - turn
to the back to see
just a few . . .

I have always been a teacher, or so it seems . . .
I used to be one of those children who made books for their teddies, thought up sums for them and then wrote in the answers!

I loved teaching.

When I became a teacher I found it easy. Which is why it came as a big shock when I found it hard to teach my own children.

They didn't want me to be a teacher, they wanted me to be mummy.

No matter how much I insisted that I could show them a quick way to do something they replied that they didn't want my help as it was not the way they did it in school.

I realized that as a parent I had to find a different way to teach them so that they didn't know it was a lesson.

Teaching through playing games was the way forward.

Teaching through playing games was,
and still is the way forward.

The games must be fun.

You must look as though you are having fun . . .
even if you have 100 other things you could be
doing.

The games must be short.

That way you'll both want to play again.

Playing games will give your child
the confidence they need to enjoy learning
Maths and English.

Parents often say . . .

I can't help my child.

I wasn't very good at maths.

My child doesn't understand number bonds.

I find it hard to know how to help.

My child can't learn their tables.

How can I help with storywriting?

Children often say . . .

I know my tables . . .
   when in fact they can only count in multiples.

I find problem solving difficult.

I can't do sums with weights and measures.

I know what I want to write, but I find it hard to get it down on paper.

This can mean that . . .

When children find one concept difficult to understand they can lose their confidence.

They may feel unable to ask for help at school.

They might be afraid that they will look stupid and think that they are the only one in the class that can't understand.

Once they fall behind they are likely to drop further behind, particularly with maths which is a building block subject.

You may feel unable to help because, either your child finds it difficult to explain which bit they don't understand, or you didn't like the subject.

Putting the fun back into learning will break the cycle, rebuild confidence and increase ability.

Here are some ideas and games to play at home, which may help to boost confidence.

Having Fun, Building Confidence

You'll need to blast them with confidence !

To excel at a subject, children need to feel confident in their abilities. The best way to boost a child's confidence is to make the subject fun.

Make them feel special by giving them . . .

1. A comfy place to play the game.

2. A treat, such as a warm drink. I find hot chocolate works wonders.

3. Give them a sense of fun and your entire attention.

4. Make up a good name for a pretty ordinary game. You want them to sit down and learn addition, so call the counters 'monkeys' and call it the Funky Monkey Game! They might be more likely to want to learn addition!

A happy child learns more easily.

Making

Maths

Fun

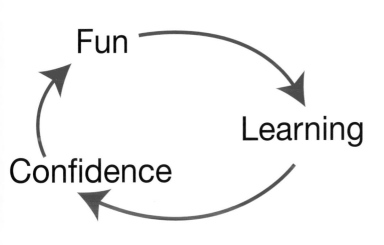

Fun

Learning

Confidence

Teaching . . . Counting On

$$7 + 2 = 9$$

'Counting on' means just looking at one number, and only counting on the other number.

Young children will usually look at the first number, go back and count all the way up from 1 to 7 . . . and then count on 2 more to make 9.

Children should be able to just look at 7 and only count on 2 to make 9.

Games To Play:

1. Addition Game

2. Shut the Box

3. Any board game that uses 2 dice

The Addition Game

Use this board.
Up to 10 counters and 2 dice . . .
(1 with dots
1 with numbers)

9	3	7	5
4	10	6	9
2	5	11	8
7	10	3	12
6	4	8	5

1. The first player throws both dice.
2. They say the answer on the numbered one, and then count on the number of dots on the 'ordinary' dice.
   For example 5 + ⚁ = 7
3. A counter is placed on the answer.
4. The second player does the same and places their counter.

The winner is the first person to get rid of all their counters.

The person who starts usually wins!

Shut the Box

For 2 or more players
Write out numbers 1 - 9
2 dice and 1 pencil

1 2 3 4 5 6 7 8 9

1. First person rolls the dice and adds them together. (⚃ count on ⚁ makes 8)
2. Cross 8 off your list.
3. Same person rolls the dice again, adds the numbers and again crosses the answer off the list.
4. If you roll an answer that has already been crossed off, try and find another way to make that number. (1 + 7 = 8, 2 + 6 = 8, 3 + 5 = 8)
5. Use both dice until the only numbers not crossed off are 5 or under. Then you can use one dice.
6. Continue until you can't cross off any more. Add the remaining uncrossed numbers. They are your score.

The winner is the person with the lowest score!

Teaching . . . Number Bonds

It is really important to know instantly which numbers go together to make another number . . . without having to work it out.

6 and 4 make 10

This is part of a solid foundation that will give a child confidence with maths.

Games To Play:

1. Shut The Box

2. Darts

3. Maths Challenge

Darts

You'll need a dartboard and 3 darts.
If you are playing with a very young child
you may prefer a magnetic dartboard.

1. Establish the safety rules.
2. You throw all 3 darts. The child adds the numbers and writes down the score.
3. Your child throws all 3 darts, adds the numbers and writes down the score.
4. The winner is the person with the highest score.

This is an excellent way to teach Number Bonds.
Show your child easy ways to add big numbers.
(To add 19 . . . you add 20 and then take away 1)

If your child miscalculates, look really pleased and say that you didn't think that you had done that well . . . they'll soon get the hint and do the sum again!

It's an easy way to teach that accuracy matters!

Maths Challenge

Make a pack of up to 52 cards.
If you want the game to be shorter . . .
use fewer cards.

Write a sum on each card. The answers should all be 10 or under.

7 - 2	4 + 6	3 + 0	9 - 5

1. The shuffled pack is placed face down on the table.
2. You each take a card.
3. Your child does both sums.
4. The person with the highest answer takes both cards.
5. If the cards have the same answer, they are placed to one side. At the end of the game the winner of the last pair takes those cards.

Encourage your child to just look at the sum and say the answer.

Teaching . . . Times Tables

Knowing your tables is an essential part of having confidence with maths.

It's all very well being able to count up in multiples, but it won't give your child the speed that they will need for tests and exams.

To be able to give the answer instantly inspires confidence, and with that confidence comes speed and ultimately success.

Games To Play:

1. Mrs J's Brilliant Tables Games

2. The Clicking Clicker Game

3. Dominoes . . . but not as you know it

Mrs J's Brilliant Tables Games

There are two versions of the game both of which a child can play by themselves. One is a brightly coloured card game, and the other is an app. Both are fun and crucially do not rely on counting or guesswork. They are multi-sensorial using touch, sight and hearing.

They teach the question and the answer which need to be learned together so that a child can say instantly, and with confidence, that 7 x 8 = 56.

Tables learning can be easy and fun!

Each Table can be practiced at 6 different levels. The beginners can start with answers up to 5 . . . and graduate through the levels until they are confident enough to do the whole Times Table and all the answers up to 12.

More details about both the game and the app can be found on the website: mrsj.edenkent.org

These games really work!

The Clicking Clicker Game

For 2 or 3
players
1 'pop up' dice
10 counters each

8	24	15	6	36	15
30	5	9	3	20	6
12	12	20	4	30	4
6	2	6	16	18	10
12	2	8	1	24	12
25	3	18	5	10	4

1. The first player clicks the dice, and then does it again. (If you have not got a 'pop up' dice just throw a normal one.)
2. The two numbers are multiplied together.
3. A counter is placed on the answer.
4. The second player does the same and places their counter.
5. The winner is the first person to get rid of all their counters.
6. To make the game more exciting you can win early by placing your counters on four numbers to form a square shape.

The person who starts usually wins!

Times Tables Dominoes

2 players

This is a really good game for teaching that anything x 0 = 0

1. Lay out the dominoes face down.

2. Take one domino each.

3. Turn them over and multiply the two numbers together. (5 x 2 = 10)

4. The person with the highest score takes both dominoes.

5. If both answers are the same leave them to one side.

   6 x 2 = 12   4 x 3 = 12

6. At the end of the game the winner of the last pair also takes those dominoes.

The winner is the person with the most dominoes at the end of the game!

Teaching Coordinates

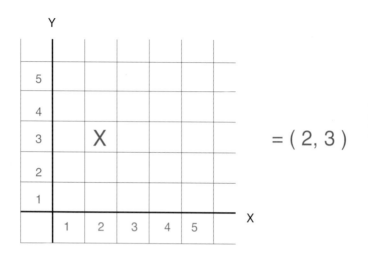

The X coordinate (along) is written first, then the Y coordinate (up).

'Along the corridor and up the stairs' is a helpful way to remember.

Games To Play:

1. Three in a Row Game

2. Battleships

3. Find the Treasure Game

Three in a Row Game

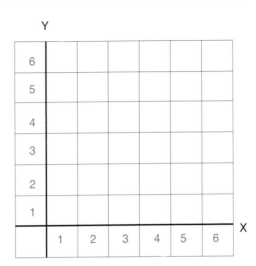

For 2 players.
Use this board,
2 dice (They must
be different colours)
10 counters each.

1. Decide which colour dice to always read first.

2. Throw both dice.

3. Look at the number on your first dice. That will be the number along the bottom. The second number will be the one up the side. Put a counter in this position on the board.

The winner is the first to get three in a row, or in a column, or on a diagonal.

Battleships

You will need this board and a paper version.

- • • • • Four counters for an aircraft carrier
- • • • Three counters for a battleship
- • • Two counters for a destroyer
- • • Two counters for another destroyer

Battleships continued . . .

1. One player 'hides' their ships on the board by placing them in rows, columns or diagonals.

2. The other player has a paper copy of the board and a pencil. They call out a coordinate.

3. If there is a ship in that place on the board the player must call out 'HIT'.
   If not they call out 'SPLASH'.

4. The player with the pencil marks their paper copy with an X for a 'HIT'
   or a --- for a SPLASH.

5. When all the ships have been sunk the players swap places.

The winner is the player who used fewer coordinates to sink all their opponents' ships!

Find the Treasure Game

Make 2 paper copies
of the Battleships or
Three in a Row Board.

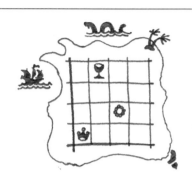

1. One person 'hides' the treasure by drawing up to 10 pieces in some of the squares.
   The treasure can be cups, necklaces, crowns, gold bars etc.

2. The other player calls out a coordinate.

3. The first person must say if 'treasure' has been found in that place.

4. The other player marks their paper copy with an X for 'TREASURE'
   or a --- for NO TREASURE.

5. Continue until all the 'treasure' has been found.

The winner is the person who found the other's 'treasure' in the fewest number of goes!

Making

English

Fun

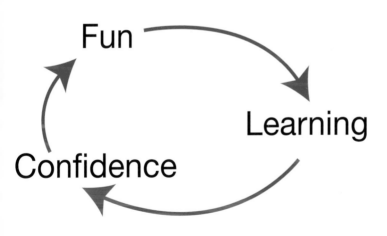

Fun

Learning

Confidence

Teaching . . . Handwriting

There are things you can do without having to ask a child to spend time copying out text neatly. Many children hate it, and it may not make a huge difference to their usual handwriting.

There are a variety of different reasons why a child's handwriting might be difficult to read. Some children deliberately write badly so that their spelling will be given the benefit of the doubt.

Others may be using a peculiar grip . . . perhaps they have been encouraged to sit and write before their hands are big enough or strong enough to hold a pencil with just three fingers. Although it is perfectly possible to have lovely handwriting with a different grip, it can be tiring and necessitate involving the whole hand or even the whole arm.

Some children even have to stop every so often and shake out their hand.

Teaching . . . Handwriting

Try Lego. The action of breaking up and building small pieces of Lego strengthens the fingers needed for writing. Have a competition where your child has to make something. You get 3 goes to guess what it is that they have constructed.

Try plasticine or playdough. Give your child small pieces to roll up into little balls using their thumb and first two fingers.

Try a 'Message Hunt'. The child writes and hides a message trail. They give you the first clue. It might say, 'Where you put your head at night'. You go to your pillow and find the next clue.
It might say, 'I can see the road'.
You find the next clue by a window . . . and so on.

There could be a small prize, a sweet or something, hidden at the end which the child keeps if you have managed to read and follow all their clues. This will remind your child that there is little point in writing if it cannot be read !

Reading to your Children

It is really important that your child reads daily.
It is just as important that you read to them.

Try choosing a book that would be too hard for them to read by themselves. It will make it different, more exciting and hopefully spur them on to improve their own reading skills.

Listening to stories allows a child to use their imagination.

Listening to stories will increase their vocabulary and even help them to understand grammar and the use of punctuation.

Audio books can also work well.

Spelling

Some children are naturally good spellers, others find it much harder. For those children it often helps to break up the word into syllables.

Write out the word to be learned.

Brill   i   ant

Give your child a sparkly pen and ask them to make each bit a different colour.

Brill   i   ant

Encourage them to read the word in the syllables, rather than trying to spell each letter individually.

This is particularly helpful for those who get lost in the middle of long words.

They are now learning a series of very short words instead of one very long word.

Teaching Language and Vocabulary

It is so important for children to be encouraged to use their own imagination without it all being served up on a plate, as film and television tend to do. These games may help.

Games to Play:

1. The Alien Game

2. The Noun Game

3. The Adjective Game

4. The Adverb Game

5. The Sound Game

6. Sights, Sounds, Feelings, Smells

The Alien Game

You are an 'Alien'.
You have no idea what things are, so you ask,
"What is a sock?"
or anything else that comes to mind.

Your child has to explain, using words only, in such a way so that you know it isn't a slipper, a pair of tights or even a shoe. Just saying that it goes on your foot is not enough.

Feel free to be a friendly, but completely clueless 'Alien' and ask as many questions as you like!

This is useful for playing in the car or on trains and in buses. Many children know the answer to comprehension questions but find it difficult to get it down on paper.

This game helps with all forms of writing as it enables a child to answer questions clearly and succinctly.

The Noun Game

Make a list of adjectives and take it in turns to think of a noun to go with them.

A generous   man, gift, thought

A deep   pond, sleep, cut

A narrow   path, escape, ribbon

A sour   apple, look, sweet

A miserable   time, afternoon

A wide   gap, smile, river

A troublesome   dog, tooth, sum

This is another good game to play while travelling or waiting for an appointment.

The Adjective Game

Decide what you want to describe.

A Cloud (or anything else that comes to mind)

Each person takes turns to think of a word that
could describe a cloud . . .

White   Fluffy   Big   Thunderous

It doesn't have to be the same cloud!

If you join in they will remember your 'good' word
and use it next time you play or, hopefully, in a
story.

This game is helpful for those children whose
essays and stories are of the . . .
. . . 'and then he did this, and then he did that' . . .
variety.
This may add a bit of description to their writing.

The Adverb Game

Make a list of verbs and ask your child
to think of ways to do them.

Shouted	loudly, desperately, angrily
Decided	eventually, suddenly, bravely
Smiled	happily, sneeringly, shyly
Crept	quietly, stealthily, warily
Explained	carefully, vaguely, earnestly
Waited	impatiently, anxiously, fearfully
Answered	immediately, politely, softly

Choose a verb and take turns thinking of as many
adverbs as possible before moving on to the next.

The Sound Game

Make a list of sounds and ask your child
to think of anything that would make that noise.

The rustle of	leaves, newspaper
The rumble of	thunder, a train
The hiss of	a snake, steam
The patter of	feet, raindrops
The buzz of	a doorbell, a chainsaw
The creak of	a hinge, a floorboard
The clatter of	dishes, hooves

Take turns thinking of as many different things
as possible before moving on to the next.

Sights, Sounds, Feelings, Smells

This game helps with story writing.
It slows down the action and adds description.
Decide where you want to be:
> In a garden
> At the supermarket
> Out for a walk
> In the kitchen
> At the seaside . . . etc.

Ask the child to imagine, and then list:

1. Sights . . .   What can you see?

2. Sounds . . . What can you hear?

3. Feelings . . . What can you feel?
                          How do you feel?

4. Smells . . .   What can you smell?

The next time they have to write about any of
these places they will have instant vocabulary.

Other

Good

Games

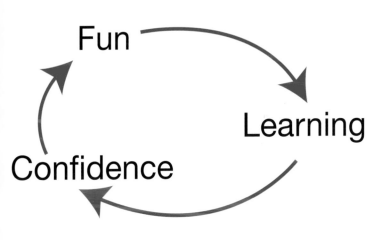

Fun

Learning

Confidence

Memory Games

These are really good games that will increase memory particularly for those children who find it difficult to remember sequences and information that hasn't been experienced.

They will work well even with very young children.

Games To Play:

1. Find the Twin Game

2. Pelmanism

Find the Twin Game

Start with 3 pairs of cards such as SNAP cards.

1. Make up a story about 6 friends who have come to tea and after tea they all go for a long walk.
2. Take the cards for a 'walk' and leave one of each pair somewhere in the room.
3. Then ask the child to help find the 3 missing 'friends'.
4. Show the child one of the cards and ask them to find the missing one which looks exactly the same.

For very young children you may like to continue the story by saying, "They put on their big brown boots and went into a deep, dark forest" . . . etc. as the child is finding the 'friend'.

Later you can make the game more difficult by placing the cards in another room, making the cards quite similar, or adding more cards.

Pelmanism

You will need a pack of SNAP cards.

Start with 10 cards. (5 matching pairs)
Lay them out face down.

The idea is to remember where the pairs are
and take them off the table.

1. The first person chooses a card and turns it
   over leaving it in the same position on the
   table. They do the same with a second card.

2. If the cards are a pair they take them and
   have another go. If they are not a pair they
   are replaced, face down, on the table.

3. The second person chooses a card and turns
   it face up. If they know where its pair is, they
   try to find it.

The winner is the person with the most pairs
at the end !

And finally . . .

Jigsaw puzzles, measuring out ingredients when cooking and water toys in the bath are also great activities.

They will all help to give confidence and remind your child that learning can be fun.

Teaching at home through playing games is the way forward.

Here they are!

Also -
Many thanks to H and Dj for their endless
encouragement and all those who helped with
proof reading.

If you found this book useful and would like a
few more copies for friends and relatives
email:-   mrsjrules@hotmail.co.uk
or go to:-   mrsj.edenkent.org